What I love about

GRANDMA

1

I love it when we go

____

together.

2

Your

____

is really beautiful.

3

I love eating

____

with you.

4

When I see

____

I always think of you.

5

I love that

____

you always wear.

6

You cook the best

____

in the world.

7

I love to

____

for you.

8

I have so much fun when we

____

together.

9

Your

____

really inspires me.

10

When you

____

I can really feel your love.

11

Your

____

is kind of adorable.

12

I love that you tell me how

____

I am.

13

I've never met anyone as

____

as you.

14

I love spending

with you.

15

You'd definitely win a

____

competition.

16

I love it when you and I

____

together.

17

The word

____

doesn't even begin to describe you.

18

I love it when we

____

We should do it more often!

19

I hope to be as

____

as you are when I grow up.

20

I loved

____

with you when I was little.

21

When I smell

____

it reminds me of you.

22

I love watching

____

with you.

23

I love to

____

when we go visit you.

24

You're the best

____

in the world.

25

I love you because you're

____

inside and out.

26

I love your

____

27

You're sweeter than

____

28

Thank you for teaching me to

____

29

I love it when you call me

30

Thank you for giving me

____

31

I love your stories about

____

32

I'll never forget when we went to

____

33

I love to make you laugh by

____

34

When you hug me, I feel

____

35

I love that you're so

____

36

When we're together

____

37

I love that you love my

____

38

You have the best

____

39

I love your contagious

____

40

Your heart is

____

41

I love it when you spoil me by

____

42

Thank you for making me feel

____

43

I love hearing about your

____

44

I love you because our relationship is

____

45

You look ______________________

when you wear ________________

46

The way you ____________________

always makes me ________________

47

I love that your ____________________

is so _________________________________

48

If you were a ______________________________

you'd be ______________________________

49

I love you more than ___________

loves _________________________

50

Thank you for

I hope you liked the book and
that you'll keep it as a reminder
of how much you mean to me!

Printed in Great Britain
by Amazon

33592879R00063